Book Signing Party
A Writer's Marketing System for Book Selling Success

JASON MOSER

Book Signing Party – A Writer's Marketing System for Book Selling Success

ISBN-13: 978-1502382658

ISBN-10: 1502382652

Copyright © 2019 by Jason Moser
505 Thorneloe Lane
Chesapeake, VA 23320

Cover designed by Jason Moser

Published by Jason Moser
505 Thorneloe Lane
Chesapeake, VA 23320

1st printing, Hardcopy and Kindle, October 2014
2nd printing, Hardcopy and Kindle, September 2019

DEDICATION

This book is dedicated to all of the authors out there struggling to make money with your writing. By immersing yourself in direct sales (but by using a comfortable approach) with your book, you'll be able to sell more books and realize your writing dreams like never before.

TABLE OF CONTENTS

INTRODUCTION

As a writer with a newly published book, it is very important for the success of your book to make a lot of sales within the first few months of publication. You want to get the marketing ball rolling as quickly as possible. In order to reach this goal, you require a bit of marketing knowledge and skills, something most authors do not have. The proven and most powerful marketing tool available to all writers, new and experienced alike, is the all dreaded book signing.

Book signings provide an author and book with two essential marketing fuels:

1. Direct exposure of your book to a market.

2. Direct exposure between the reader and the author, greatly improving the chance to make a sale.

There are also many other benefits of holding book signings. You make immediate sales putting money directly into your pocket; readers are more willing to purchase a book when they meet the author in person; it's an opportunity for you to hand out marketing materials to help build viral referral marketing opportunities; you build your reputation around the community as an author; you build a relationship with your readers that fosters repeat or future sales.

The list goes on and on.

But there are just a couple reasons why authors don't fully utilize book signings to their full potential as a means of effective book marketing. Primarily for new authors, a book signing may be intimidating. Besides not knowing most of the people you sell books to, you don't exactly know how to sell your book (because you aren't a salesman, you are an author). What do you say? How do you act? What do you wear? How do you sign the book? How do you get people to your signing? There are so many things to think about – or worry about – if you haven't held a book signing before.

This book is about to even up the playing field and actually give authors a real chance at book marketing success. *Book Signing Party* introduces a new way authors can successfully tap into this powerful marketing source while mitigating many of the difficulties faced by authors and taking full advantage of the marketing aspect of book signings.

A book signing party is much like a traditional book signing, but with an amazing twist that makes them much easier to handle for a writer and has a lot more earning and future referral marketing potential. As an entrepreneur, I was involved with many marketing presentations that used in-home sales systems and marketing models to push sales. In fact, it is the preferred way to introduce your friends and family to the products you are offering. These models are so successful, they drive billions of dollars in revenue for network marketing companies every year. These companies (Avon, Mary Kay, Amway, Quixtar, Isagenix, etc…) created a great system that is easily duplicated and within the capabilities of the most junior sales representative.

My thought while trying to break the marketing code for writers was simple: why can't an author hold a sales party for their product at their home or other people's homes? Instead of dumping an author out of their comfort zone and throwing them into book stores and book shows, let them stay or at least start out within their comfort zone, and do the book signings and readings for their friends and family members. After a couple of parties, open up the playing field a little and hold signing parties at friend's homes, allowing you to reach new networks of motivated buyers.

Once the author is comfortable talking to people about their book, then they can extend their reach within the community and hold a public book signing at a local book store. By starting out within your comfort zone, you ease your way into the marketing world more readily and more effectively, thus learning valuable skills and techniques you will need when taking on real book signings and book marketing events in public.

Book Signing Party will provide you with the foundation, the system, needed to jump start your book sales right out of the gate. It will walk you through how to invite guests, prepare for a party, conduct the party, and effectively set yourself up with more parties to tap into other people's networks.

Guests invited to a sales party are highly motivated to buy your book. They already have a relationship with you, one of the main reasons why in home sales presentations are so successful. Most of your guests will purchase a book (if not two), and will be more open to buy future books that you write just because they know YOU are the author.

Most writers are very quiet about what they do. Most of their friends don't even know they write. Inviting them to a book signing at your home will certainly enlighten them to the fact and you may be pleasantly surprised with their response. And most of them will want to support your writing once they find out because now you are a celebrity that they personally know.

You are in control of your book's destiny and your direction as an author. Aggressive marketing is essential to book selling success. Follow *Book Signing Party – A Writer's Marketing System for Book Selling Success* for a powerful start in the right direction.

Jason Moser
Author and Entrepreneur

GETTING YOUR BOOK AND YOUR NAME OUT THERE

Your Initial Marketing Efforts after You Publish a Book

Even before you have a book signing, you need to get your initial marketing efforts out of the way. Marketing is a combined sales and distribution avenue you use to push your product (in this case, your book). When you launch any product, you want to get the word out very quickly that it's out there and ready for the world to buy.

The reason you want to get started marketing right away is because this is when you are the most excited about that product and this is what fuels your motivation to continue marketing months later.

When a publisher gives you an advance for publishing your book, they are giving you the money to free up your time and to help fund your initial marketing efforts. You have to pay that advance back through the sales of your book. Sometimes an author will get an advance large enough to stop working for a year so they can dedicate all of their time to book marketing. The goal is to get enough book sales in order to pay back your advance and start a viral effect for your book that won't stop.

Some of the problems with most authors are that they are afraid to sell their book directly, they don't know how to sell their book, or they do nothing as far as marketing is concerned once their book is published. If you do nothing, you will make nothing from your book. The more you do, the more you will make. The point is, as an author, your job is not done when you are finished writing and publishing your book. You **MUST** put forth the effort to sell your book in order to make money from it. No one else is going to do it for you.

Before your book is published and released to the public, you should make some announcements to let people know it is coming. Your social networks (Facebook, Twitter, Google+, LinkedIn, and more) are your first place to turn to in order to make these announcements of upcoming release of your book. Making these deadline announcements keeps your goals for publishing on track and people will keep an eye out for future announcements. Blogs and forums are another great social reach for announcing your book release date.

Prior to publishing your book, it is also a good idea to create a search engine optimized website for you and your book(s). If you don't already have one, a website is a critical part of your marketing mix and is essential to the success of your marketing campaigns. Where are you going to send people if you are trying to sell a book, especially if it isn't published yet? Your website is a virtual base of operations where all of your other marketing methods feed into to get the sale or future sale.

When first going public with your book after you publish, you should always hit up your social networking sites with a book announcement first. Direct sales are usually a no no on social media platforms, but you can direct people to visit your website for more information. You should always include a picture of the cover of your book, where they can make the purchase (a link to your website), and a short sentence or two about your book. You can also add a link to a sample chapter of your book so long as they can purchase your book after they read it. Social networking for the most part is free (they do offer paid advertising to the network, but that is not necessary just yet).

After your social marketing push, you need to make your announcement through media press releases on and off line. Local media outlets want local news and you publishing a book, no matter what type, is a big deal. And there are literally thousands of media sources online that will run your press release. You still need to tell people how to find your book and an author website is the best place to start.

Press releases to the media vary based on the source, but there are a lot of them you can solicit and run your release on for free in exchange for an interview. There are also some press release outlets that send your release to a network of media sources, but these generally can cost some money. These are well worth the expense if you don't know how to get your press release out to the media and want it circulated throughout the country.

Now, back to your book or author website. If a publisher publishes your book, you will get a small (one to three page) website that has your book, a buy button, and maybe a couple of reviews and such. The only problem with these websites is that they are not going to rank very high in the search engines and no one will ever find you or your book online if they do a search in Google, Bing, or Yahoo. You want more than just a place to send people to buy your books – you want a place people can find on their own if they are looking for a book with content such as yours.

In online marketing, search engine marketing is your biggest source of potential customers in the world, and besides the cost of the domain name, hosting, and the time to maintain a website, it can become the most profitable source of eyes on your book. Of course you must have more than one or two pages of content for your website. They also need to be search engine friendly and optimized to magnetically attract people to your website.

Now that you have a good base for your marketing engine, your next step is some sales that are more direct. That's where book signings come into play. A book signing is great because you purchase your books at wholesale (or cost of the book) and you sell them for retail at your book signings. The income you earn at a book signing is immediate and you don't have to pay any middlemen a piece of your profits, unless of course you do a book signing at a book store and they want so much percent of your sales.

A book signing party in your own home is a great alternative because you don't have to pay a percentage of your sales to the store owner. You can give incentives to people who host a book signing party at their house for you, but generally people will do it for nothing just to help out. And the marketing efforts to get people to your in-home book signing are totally different than the efforts for a public book signing.

You will see the many marketing advantages for a book signing party vice a public book signing event as you continue reading.

ESTABLISHING YOUR GOALS

Before you even consider having a book signing party in your home, you must create a fool proof plan. A plan is the blueprint for your party. Your primary goal is simple: it is to have a successful book signing party. But in order for your signing to be successful, you need to establish goals associated with that party that lead up to the end result.

Goals should always be written down and contain enough information to help you achieve that goal.

Here are the three parts each goal should have:

1. Description of what you wish to accomplish.

2. Specifics – dates, numbers of guests, number of sales, etc…

3. Deadline or accomplishment metric. When will it be completed or what justifies accomplishment of that goal.

In traditional goal writing, there is a fourth part – a reward. I usually add in a reward to all of my goals for added motivation, but all of these goals are aiming for the same end result (your primary objective of having a successful book signing). Your primary objective should have a reward for successful completion at a minimum, but it will not be necessary for the smaller goals leading up to the primary one.

Below is an example of a primary objective goal:

"I will have a successful book signing party at my home on *date* at *time*. I will have ### guests that attend who purchase at least ### books for a total of $$$$$$ in sales. When I achieve this goal, I will reward myself with a *something you really want and will motivate you to reach your goals*."

After this primary goal is written, you will need to create a series of smaller goals that will lead up to the accomplishment of this goal and ultimately a successful signing.

How many guests will you need to invite to get one to show up? This number varies based on your friends and family and their availability when you plan to have your party. When do you have to have all of your invitations out in order to receive RSVPs for the party to confirm your guests? How many books do you buy or have on hand for the event? When should you follow up with all of your guests?

There are a lot of factors that go into planning a book signing party. Initially, there may be a little more costs involved with purchasing marketing materials, food, beverages, and gifts, but anything left over can be used for a few more book signing parties so nothing is ever going to be wasted.

The easiest way to come up with this series of goals is to write down everything you can think of regarding the book signing party. Prioritize everything and start writing out your goals. Once all of your goals are written, it's good to generate a "To Do List" in the order you need to accomplish everything so you can successfully manage your time and get all of your goals done on time for the party.

If you think of anything you can add to your goal list after you are done writing all of your goals out, just write them down and add them to your list in the appropriate time frame. This is just a guide and motivational tool, so it isn't life-shattering if you forget a detail or two.

BOOK SIGNING PARTY BUDGET

Marketing your book will always cost you money one way or another. The efficiency of your dollar is what makes your marketing campaigns effective. If you use your money for website clicks from a search engine's pay per click system, the visitor clicking that link is usually just browsing around and will not buy your book. They are cold leads.

When you personally invite someone into your home for a book signing party, since you already know them (or the person who allows you to hold a book signing in their house knows them), they are warm or hot leads. Hot leads will buy your book almost every time. Would you rather put a hundred dollars toward a cold lead that probably won't buy your book or a hundred dollars toward a handful of hot leads that will most likely buy your book? Which one will give you a better return on investment?

$$\textbf{ROI (Return on Investment)} = \textbf{Invest / Revenue}$$

$$\textbf{ROI} = \$100 / \$250 = 40\% \textbf{ ROI}$$

Putting all of your money up front into one marketing bucket isn't a very smart thing to do when you look at your book as an investment, even if it is a sure thing. You need to spread that investment around into several marketing buckets to get as many eyes on your book as possible, but you need to be smart about where that money goes. Since you are using your budget mostly for marketing, you need to determine which sources will be the most profitable, not only in the short term, but the long term.

Return on investment (ROI) is very important to an author, especially one with little to no money to start out with. That's why you start your marketing efforts with social networking. This is your best **FREE** source of immediate income. It will also help fund your budget for some paid advertising programs.

You must think about your book selling as a business. When you make $5.00 from a couple of book sales, you don't take that money and spend it on a cup of coffee at Starbucks. No yet, anyways. You take that $5.00 and apply it to your writing budget so you can use it for more marketing to make more money to roll back into your budget.

The concept is called compounding. It is easy, but people don't always follow this rule. They spend the money and complain that they don't have any money to use for marketing.

With that said, you may need to make a personal investment in your business to get the ball rolling. Book signing parties aren't free. For a successful party, you need to spend a little money on a handful of things. Most items that don't perish (like food) can be bought in bulk and used for more than one party. And in order to get the ball rolling, you will need to have a little money in your budget to start with.

If you don't know how a budget works, here's a quick rundown:

Income: Money that you personally invest or make from book sales revenue. You can also make some extra or side income from your website (Adsense ads and affiliates).

Expenses: Amount of money needed to buy books. Money paid out for online advertising. Money for business cards. Money for post cards. Money for postage. Money for shipping envelopes. Money for address labels. Money for book signing essentials.

You take your income and subtract your expenses. The remaining amount left over is either a **surplus** (you make more than you spend) or **deficit** (negative amount – you spend more than you make). You always want a surplus when dealing with your budget. Don't spend more than you have.

A book signing budget has its own parts for the expenses. Each party may be a little different, but generally there are a few things you must buy in order to maximize your party's chances of success.

Some of the typical expenses are shown below:

1. Invitations
2. Envelopes
3. Postage
4. Thank you cards
5. Posters (for decoration)
6. Book marks (for handouts)
7. Gifts to give to guests (Gift cards, coupons, other books you wrote…)
8. Pens for signing
9. A guest book (for tracking your attending guest's)
10. Food (snacks for your guests)
11. Beverages (soda, tea, juice for your guests)
12. Gift Bags
13. Childcare (baby sitter(s))
14. Banner (for decoration)
15. Everything else you spend money on directly related to your book signing.

Depending on what all you do for the party will determine how much you need to spend. You will be able to better come up with numbers for your budget based on how many guests you invite, how many respond, how many books you need to buy and so on.

Keeping track of the numbers is what your budget is all about. It's important for you as a book seller to not go in the red. This is a de-motivator that can stop your marketing efforts in their tracks. Once you make some profits with a successful book signing party, future budgets will be easy. Just remember to reinvest your earnings. Your compounded efforts will grow exponentially with your continued investment.

PLANNING A BOOK SIGNING PARTY

The Book Signing Party System is a simple program to help you organize and plan a successful book signing event. With a little bit of guidance, you will have all the knowledge you need to throw together a successful signing party.

There are several considerations for you book signing. Everything will be explained throughout this chapter. A link to a planning checklist is included at the back of the book for a handy reference while planning your in-home book signing event.

You will also read some examples with numbers from case studies and trials. Not all book signings are equal and success for each party cannot be guaranteed. The more signings you host, the more organized and well planned they will be.

So, take lots of notes while you are conducting a party (during every stage from planning to completion) and keep track of what is working and what isn't working. Things that aren't working very well can be omitted or modified to improve their success. Just like with anything you do, the more you do it, the better at it you will become.

Planning your book signing party is essential if you want it to be successful. You should have already established your goals and have your budget laid out. Now it's time to establish a plan for your party.

For considerations of your plan, you will need a calendar and you will have to be able to manage your time. Since it will take some time to get invites out, receive purchased books, receive responses to your invites, and to get your marketing materials made up, you will want to plan your party far enough out to make sure you have everything for the party (especially your books).

The following considerations will need to be determined for your plan:

1. Number of Guests to Invite.
2. Number of Books to Purchase.
3. Type and Number of Gifts to Get for Your Guests.
4. Types and Number of Marketing Materials to Purchase.
5. What Games are You Going to Have to Entertain Your Guests?
6. Types of Props for Your Party.
7. Types of Food and Beverages for Your Party.
8. Types of Signing Materials.
9. Making a Schedule of Events for Your Party.
10. Methods for Child Care for Guests.
11. How to Follow Up With Your Guests and People That Can't Attend.
12. How to Get Others to Hold Parties at Their Homes.
13. How Guests Going to Get to Your Party.
14. Where People are Going to Park.

With these considerations in mind, you need to organize them on a timeline and figure out how much time is needed for all of the materials, gifts, books, and anything else that has to be made or ordered in order to arrive in time for the party. You also want to carefully choose a date for your party. Pick a weekend (Sunday afternoon is probably the best time, but Saturday's will work too) if you can, but evenings after dinner will work too. You want to choose a time that is good for as many people as possible. You can't accommodate everyone, so don't kill yourself over this part of your plan.

It's important to stick to your plan once a day and time is set and the party is in motion. That means once you decide to hold a book signing party in your home, you must follow through. Once those invites go out, you can't stop the marketing ball from rolling. It may be a little outside the box for you, but you can't succeed if you don't take things a little further than where you are right now.

Now that you know the considerations of a book signing party, you will learn more in detail about each consideration and why they are important for your party.

GETTING PEOPLE TO YOUR PARTY

Getting people to your party is usually the most difficult part of the whole process. But, this isn't some network marketing company your guests have probably heard negative things about from friends or relatives. This is your own personalized product, a book, written from your heart and soul – entertainment. This is different from vitamins, weight loss programs, make up, and soap. This is actually totally different and thus easier than those other company's in home parties.

A book is a very unique and personalized product. When you invited your friends and family to a party, they don't know anything about your book (unless they already bought it or you told them about it) and they are either curious or supportive if they say "yes" to your invite. So, getting people to your party is not very difficult at all.

Getting guests in your home is all about networking. It's all about who you know! Now, you may not think you know a lot of people, but let me tell you, if you really dig down deep, you do know at least 250 people.

When determining who to invite, you must first have a list of people in which to "pull" from. Building your initial networking list may take some time, but it will be well worth it in the long run and provide you with several parties for the months to come.

I created a program called The Keep in Touch program over the years and it helps organize your network of friends, family, and other people you know. Here's a basic rundown of how it works.

The Keep in Touch Program

You want to create an extensive list of everyone you know. This list contains four parts:

List A: These are the people who you know very well, correspond with regularly in person, phone, chat, or email, and that are your family or very close friends. These are your **HOT LEADS**.

List B: These are the people who you know but don't correspond with regularly. They are acquaintances. Generally, you know how to contact them and they will know who you are when you do contact them, but they aren't close friends. They are the people you work with, talk to once or twice a year, see at the hair salon, see at functions, and others you see but don't generally hang out with on a regular basis. These are your **WARM LEADS**.

List C: These are the people you know but don't know how to get a hold of them. When you see them you will know them and recognize them. You can start a conversation with them, but you don't always go out of your way to contact them. These are old classmates from high school or college, old colleagues from work, the mail man, the milk man, the store clerk you see every day, and so on. You know their name and a little bit about them, but that's about it. Can be **WARM** or **COLD LEADS**.

List D: These are the people who either you don't want to stay in contact with or who don't want to stay in contact with you. This is your "unsubscribe list" or the people who opt out of your list, either because of a fight or for some other negative reason. You still know them and it's good to keep track of these people just so you can avoid conflict later on.

With these four parts or lists, you can develop a significantly large list of names of who you can invite to your parties.

When creating your lists, you want to break the lists up into several sections. You want to separate all of the people you know who are local and who are in other cities (but can be grouped together) where you may have to travel.

Book signing parties don't always have to be held in your home. If you live in Florida but most of your family is from Ohio, arrange a date where you can hold a book signing party in Ohio at a family member's house so all of your family can attend.

Don't leave anyone off of your list, no matter how insignificant it may seem. If you know them, write down their name and as much information you can about them. Look through your old year books, go through your social networks, go through your address book, and go through old Christmas cards. Write down everyone you know. One of your old classmates may become your biggest fan – you just never know.

The most important consideration for your book signing party is your local A List followed by your local B List. These are your hot and warm list of potential buyers and the first group of people you will be inviting to your party. Since you know how to contact these people, you can contact them and get their mailing address (if you don't already have it). It is important to have a physical mailing address for the people you invited, not only for the book signing party invites, but for other announcements and mailings in the future.

You don't just have to use your Keep in Touch lists for inviting people to your book signing. This program is good for other forms of marketing too such as book release announcements, post cards, and other mail outs to help sell your book. It helps you "keep in touch" with the people you know to maintain a strong relationship with them.

Marketing and sales depend on trust. Trust in turn comes from the relationship you have with a customer. A Keep in Touch program such as the one described helps maintain that relationship.

When planning your book signing party, don't invite **EVERYONE** at one time. If you invite 100 people from your list and all 100 respond positively (they are coming), you will have a predicament on your hands. Always start with your local A List and work your way down into your local B List. You should only invite about twenty-five people to your party at first. If they all RSVP that they are coming, you can still handle it. But, you will probably only get about five to ten people to respond and come to your party.

A good book signing party will have about ten people at the most. You don't want too many people there because you can't possibly socialize with more than that in a two hour period. But you can socialize with ten. The more personal the party is to your guests, the more in tune they will be to buy your book.

So, make a pledge to invite twenty-five people to your first party. If you only get one or two RSVPs, invite twenty-five more. Your goal is to have ten people come to your book signing party.

Now you must come up with a good invitation for your party. Post cards with your book cover on them are good. They must have a date, time, address, phone number, email address, and a little note letting them know that they must RSVP to attend. If you send the invitation in an envelope, you can also put a self addressed stamped envelope inside with your invitation to encourage RSVPs. I personally like to know whether people are going to show up or not, so I require RSVPs for everybody, even if they can't come. This engages your contacts to acknowledge your invite and respond one way or another.

If you get a response that they can't make it, you should follow-up with them with a thank you note for letting you know and a way that they can order your book. Even though they can't make your party, it doesn't mean they won't buy your book. Or, you can choose to set them aside and re-invite them to another party in the future that maybe they can attend. The more communicative you are with your list, the more responsive they will be. But always give them options if they simply can't make that particular party.

Remember, these are the people you know well and correspond with regularly anyway. They will be more supportive and responsive than those on the B and C lists. Don't be afraid to reach out to any of them – you will be pleasantly surprised at the response you get.

There is a solid method of contacting and inviting that you should use each time you plan a party. First, determine who you are going to invite. Next, send out the invitations to those potential guests. Give them up to a week to respond or RSVP to your invitation. After seven days, call or email them (if you haven't heard from them) to confirm whether they are coming or not. If they do RSVP, send out a thank you note and reminder about the party as a follow-up.

Keep your guests engaged even before they attend. Personalize your party handouts (things you hand out to everyone who attends – book marks, marketing materials, and such). This can be done with personalized gift bags with their name on them. After the party, be sure to follow-up with everyone again, thanking them for attending. Future follow-ups are important, so stay in contact with the people who attend your parties. Follow-up with them at least once every six months to let them know what is going on with you and your writing. This is especially important if you are writing another book. Let them know when it is due to be released and that they will be the first able to buy it.

In summary, create your Keep in Touch lists, concentrating right now on your A List but don't stop until everyone you know is on a list. This will take some time – more than a day – so don't be discouraged if you can only think of ten people right off the top of your head. Add more people every day until you have a large pull of people to send invitations to. Once you have at least twenty-five people on your list, set a date and get those invitations out to them.

It's good to allow about two weeks between sending the invitations out and the date of the party. This gives your guests a week to respond (be sure to put a deadline for RSVPing in your invitation) to your party invitation, that way you will get your responses more rapidly. Follow-up with all of your RSVPs and the people that don't respond, giving the people that can't make it or don't respond to the invitation an alternate way to buy your book.

Your goal is to get ten people to your first book signing party. Once you hold a party, you can raise up the number as you see fit – if you can handle more after the first party, go for it. Just don't invited more than you can handle. There's no limit to how many book signing parties you can have so all of your friends and family can eventually attend.

BUYING THE RIGHT
AMOUNT OF BOOKS FOR YOUR PARTY

The math of a book signing party is very simple since you don't have to worry too much about a lot of middle man costs. Trying to determine how many books to buy for your party is a whole other story though.

So, let's say you invited twenty-five people to your party and ten people agreed to attend. My rule of thumb is to have at least two books for every guest in case guests want to buy books for their family. Some may want to only buy one, some won't buy any, but one guest may buy three or four books.

The good thing about holding a book signing party is that you personally know all of your guests. If you run out of books, you can give them an IOU and buy some more books for them, sign them, and deliver them to them at a later date.

Let's do a little math:

10 Attending Guests

Buy 2 Books Each

Each Book Costs $3.00 x 20 = $60.00

You Sell 20 Books at $8.00 per Book = $160.00

Your Profit is $100.00

The great thing with print on demand is that you can buy as many books as you want. The more you buy at a time, the cheaper they are for you. When you personally buy your own books, you are just paying the cost of the books. When someone buys a book directly from the publisher (or print on demand company), they pay the price you set for your book (or the publisher sets for your book). You get royalties from the sale and the publisher gets a percentage of the revenue.

You may not think $100.00 is a lot of money, but I'm here to tell you, when only selling books online, you only make a $1.00 to $3.00 at the most per sale (and that's if it is electronic). It's especially difficult for self-published authors because they can't mark the price too high or no one will buy their books. Larger publishers have the advantage of mass producing books so the cost of the books and subsequent price is cheaper, however, if no one buys any books, you are out thousands of dollars and have to inventory thousands of books.

Unfortunately, a book signing party will cost some money to start. You have to buy props, marketing materials, gifts, food, beverages, and signing materials. But here's where the magic happens with your book signing party.

When you hold a party and ten people show up, you may get two of them to agree to hold a party at their home for you. When this happens, you will help them invite twenty-five people (that you don't know) each to their parties. Say ten people show up to each party for a total of twenty.

20 Attending Guests

Buy 2 Books Each

Each Book Costs $3.00 x 40 = $120.00

You Sell 40 Books at $8.00 per Book = $320.00

Your Profit is $200.00

From those two parties, you may get four more people to agree to hold a party in their homes. You can see the potential of this, right? Each time you hold a party, you have an opportunity to tap into anyone else's networks (people you may or may not know). This is called referral based marketing with a viral affect. It compounds more and more with each party you hold. And you will still be holding your own book signing parties in your own home.

An author wanting to do this full time (at least five parties a week), can bring home $500.00 per week, and this is only based on our example. It all depends on how much profit you can make per book sale as well as how many guests attend and buy books. Authors with more than one book can also have their other books on hand and sell those as well. Your book signing party may just be for book two, but say you had published book one a year earlier. Even though you are promoting book two, if you have book one available for purchase, your guests may want to buy that book too.

So, you must plan ahead and have enough books for everyone. If you can afford more books, they will cost you less. Bulk orders can really save you a lot of money, but don't go overboard. Don't buy a thousand books at the beginning and expect to sell them all in a few days. Storing your inventory is not fun, especially for books. There is special storage requirements to take into account to keep the books from getting damaged. They also take up precious space in your home as well.

Regardless of how many books you need for a party, you should always carry ten books in your personal inventory at any given time in case someone wants to randomly buy your book. When someone wants to buy it and they have to wait, they may pass on it. Always carry a couple in your car, at work, and at home. You never know when the conversation will come up and they will want to buy your book.

Your main objective of a book signing isn't to make a whole lot of money up front. You are marketing your book. The key to marketing is to get your book in front of as many people as possible. Referral based marketing is the best, and cheapest, marketing in the world. When you can start tapping into other people's networks and tapping into those people's networks, you will begin making more sales than you could ever imagine.

You can literally run your whole book signing campaign for a year, holding five parties a week and bring home $10,400 based on our example. This isn't counting any other referrals and side sales you make during that time from your other marketing efforts. Once the ball is moving and people start talking about you and your book, the viral marketing engine will take over and you will become a best selling author in no time.

Based on an article at Forbes.com, in 2013, $5.25 billion in annual revenue was generated from book sales at Amazon. Unfortunately, other research has shown that a majority of self-published authors don't make more than $100.00 from their book. That's because those authors don't know how to market their books. I know you want to make more than $100.00, right?

How do you think the big named authors like Stephen King make so many book sales? He doesn't have to do book signings any more. Everyone knows his name and his style of writing.

When you are just starting out, nobody knows you. The book signings you are holding are getting people to know your name and the style of books you write. The more people you directly meet, the more people will get to know you and thus buy your books. Any future books you publish may also be bought by those people. Once enough people know you and your writing, they will talk to their friends and family about you and they will buy your books too.

Sitting at home waiting for your books to sell online or through a book store is not going to get that marketing ball rolling for you. You have to do something about it. Book signing parties are a great way to get that ball rolling quickly and they don't cost you an arm and a leg if you do it right.

PROPS, GIFTS AND MARKETING MATERIALS

The key to a successful book signing party is to profit from your efforts. But like any other business out there, you may go in the red for the first couple signings until you break even and start to profit. That's because you must start somewhere and if you don't already have money coming into your writing budget, you have to build up that income first.

You won't have all of the stuff you need to throw your first party, so you have to spend a little money up front (start up expenses) to make the first party happen. Most of this money will come out of your own pocket initially (or from some of the earnings from your initial marketing efforts).

With a party comes some kind of theme or décor that you must set up to set the mood. Just like with a birthday party or Super Bowl party, your book signing party should have props to bring your event to life. When first starting out, you don't need to go all out. But as you earn more money, it's nice to have a large banner made with your name and your book title on it.

The living room, den, or great room is the perfect area to hold your event. You want the room to be large enough to comfortably hold all of your guests, your signing table, and your food/beverage table. A fold up style table is great to set up for the signing and food/beverage areas. And make sure you have enough chairs for everyone. It's more professional to have the same style of chairs for everyone, but not necessary. Fold up chairs are great because they can be stored when they are not being used and they can be used at other book signing parties in other people's homes.

Different props you can use for your signing party are posters (one or two posters of your book cover, book title, your name or a welcome message), a large banner or two, specialized table cloths that have your book cover on then (or table cloths in the same color theme as your book), and even a slide show with various excerpts from your book scrolling through on your television. Posters can add a good visual ambiance to your party and cost under $15 per poster. You want them big enough for people to see right away (19" x 27" is standard but they can come in other sizes as well. A banner will cost anywhere from $10.00 to $45.00 depending on the size.

When choosing gifts for your party, try not to spend a lot of money. You should have one gift for a door prize (usually a free book – the winner is chosen before the actual book signing takes place or a $25 gift card for a book store or Amazon.com), a gift for everyone that comes (something like a book mark with your book cover on it), and a couple extra gifts for some of the games you use for entertainment (these can be 25% off coupons they can use when they buy your book or a $10 gift card from Amazon.com).

The gifts can also relate to the subject of your book. You need to be creative, but don't spend all of your profits here. Bookmarks are a great gift for your guests. You can add your book cover design to a bookmark along with your name and contact information. Overnightprints.com offer very reasonable pricing under $50.00 for 1,000 bookmarks.

Business (or networking) Cards are a marketing must for any author and they generally don't cost that much. Vistaprint has custom services and great design ideas that cost under $20.00 for 1,000 custom full color business cards. They do run a lot of free specials, so take advantage of them while you can.

When creating business cards, you can do it one of two ways:

1. Design an author networking card with your contact information on it.

2. Design a book advertising card to hand out to market your books.

Business cards should always be handed out to all of your guests, but they are also great for handing out to everyone else you meet along your way through life too. Be sure to have a website on your card where people can find your books or your portfolio online and buy your books. Let them know if they want to check out your books, that they can just visit the website on the card and see all of your books right there.

Post cards should always be handed out to all of your guests at a party. You want to encourage your guests to tell their friends and family members about your book, so give each guest five post cards. They will cost anywhere from $5.99 to $10.00 for 50 of them from Vistaprint. This can be costly, but it is a great way to encourage referral sales.

The great thing about using services such as Vistaprint, Overnightprints.com, and other printing companies is that they will save your design. Only order enough for a couple of parties. When you get enough money from your profits, make a larger purchase so you have some on hand for future parties.

Remember, your book signing party is a marketing opportunity for your book. Get as many marketing materials in your guest's hands as you can so they can tell their friends and family about your book.

THE SCHEDULE OF EVENTS FOR YOUR PARTY

Keeping your guests engaged in the party is key to a successful party. From start to finish, you must have a plan or schedule of events that must be followed in order to accomplish everything you set out to accomplish. Allowing your schedule to slide one way or another could cost you sales, so you want to hold a professional and well-organized book signing party.

In order to keep your guests engaged in your party, you must have a detailed timeline of events. The worst thing you can do during a party is just let people do their own thing. You must keep everything on a tight schedule, from the beginning to the end of the party. This isn't a drinking and dancing party where everyone goes wild and crazy. This is a professional party where you are aiming to sell your books. Your guests must understand that and you must keep things moving so people don't get bored.

A typical book signing party should be planned out as follows:

1. Initial Welcome. When a guest shows up at your door, you will immediately greet them with a hand shake (or hug if they are close friends or family). This is where you will hand out the "everyone gets one" gift bag to show your appreciation for their going out of their way to join you for the party.

2. Social Time. This is the very beginning of your party when you get to mingle with all of the guests and all of the guests can get all of their gossip and excitement out of the way so they aren't slowing the party down later. You should allot no more than 30 minutes for social time so you don't lose track of the party while at the same time giving everyone a chance to talk for a few minutes.

3. The Introduction. This is where you, the author, calls order to the room and quiets everyone down. You tell everyone why you are holding the party, how things are going to be run, and thank them all again for attending.

4. Activity. This should immediately follow the introduction and should include your book, the main reason for the party. You should have a pre-chosen excerpt or chapter from your book that you want to read. This is where everyone gets involved. Have everyone read a paragraph until the entire excerpt has been read. Then hand out a quiz or ask some questions regarding that excerpt. The person who answers all of the questions right gets a gift.

5. Food, Beverages, and More Social Time. This is where you provide snacks and beverages for your guests. This relaxes the party a little so people can socialize again. It's also a time when you can relax a little and get ready for the signing. Go no longer than 30 minutes during this break.

6. Author Question and Answer Time. This can take anywhere from a few minutes to a half an hour depending on how many questions your guests have. Be sure to start this part of your party off by telling them what you expect. Encourage everyone to ask at least one question about the book, why you wrote it, where the idea came from, and things about you in general with respect to your writing.

7. The Sales and Signing Time. This is the most important part of your party because this is where you will make your money. This is when you give your sales pitch (not literally, but you are trying to get them to buy your book). In order for you to sign their books, they need to buy them, right? You want to organize everything perfectly at this point. Have your guests line up at your table, discuss one on one with them a little bit about your book and what you want it to say. Don't write more than a sentence per book (otherwise you will be there all night).

8. The Conclusion. This is where you will end the party. It doesn't have to be abrupt. A subtle ending with a little social interaction is great. Don't rush them out once you sign their books. Make them feel appreciated and welcome to stay as long as they would like (within reason). If you have other obligations later on, let them know so they won't take up too much of your time. Don't forget to explain to everyone why you gave them marketing materials. Also let them know if they would like to host a book signing party at their house that they will get something in return (a gift card, a percentage of your sales, a coupon for your upcoming book, etc...) . This will be discussed later.

Maintaining this schedule for each of your parties, whether they are in your home or in other people's homes is essential. It is more difficult on you if you keep changing what you will be doing at your parties. You shouldn't be inviting the same guests to every one of your parties (unless they want to come) so people won't even know that all of your parties are the same. Plus, when you buy marketing materials and props for your parties, if everything is the same every time, then you can buy bulk materials and use them over and over again.

A successful party is accomplished through a tight schedule. Stick to your schedule and you can't lose.

ENTERTAINING YOUR GUESTS – IT IS A PARTY AFTERALL

You are holding a party at your house, may it be for makeup, jewelry, or Tupperware; the commonality of each of these parties is the entertainment factor. Why do you want to entertain your guests? To keep them from getting bored and to keep them engaged. The best entertainment is something that involves everyone.

It's your party, so be very creative with the games/activities you hold for your guests. People expect to have fun at a party, so don't let them down. And when you are promoting a book at your party, what better way is there to get people involved at the party than to involve your book? A book reading may be in order to make this happen. The only thing is, you have to make it fun and entertaining, not just a boring read.

You must plan this out before the party, carefully deciding which parts of your book to read. It can be a few paragraphs of each chapter, an entire chapter, or carefully selected excerpts from your book. Do not read the end of the book! No spoilers!

A way to get everyone involved is to have everyone read a little (a paragraph or two). Then, to check who was paying attention, have a quiz afterwards, either written or spoken. Whoever gets the most questions right wins a prize.

Another activity that you can do that is fun and will get everyone involved is reading a few paragraphs and having your guests "finish the chapter". Have each person tell you how that chapter's plot is going to go. What do they think is going to happen? It's best to pick an exciting, action packed part of your book for this. Whoever comes closer to how the chapter actually goes wins a prize. The people that already bought your book and read it are exempt.

Now, some people are shy and won't want to participate. Don't force them. Don't make them feel awkward. Just pass them up and move on to the next person. Someone is going to talk and participate.

Games aren't everything at a party. You also need food and beverages. People love to snack. Just don't put all of one kind of food on a table. You should use a little bit of everything – vegetable trays, fruit trays, crackers, chips, dip, salsa, cookies, and cake are appropriate and very inexpensive.

Drinks can be a little trickier. The best thing to do is get some plastic cups and put out a pitcher of ice water, a pitcher of sweet tea, a pitcher of unsweetened tea, and a pot of coffee with the appropriate condiments. If you know your guests like soda or juice, you can use the one liter soda bottles or juice bottles too. But keep it simple.

No alcohol! Though the party may be a lot more fun with beer, wine or booze, it is not appropriate for the situation. Unless, of course, the book you are selling is how to make beer or wine, in which samples of beer or wine made with your recipes and suggestions may be appropriate.

Entertaining your guests will become easier after the first time. Asking your friends what kind of games you can do may help you come up with some great ideas as well. If you can't think up a game, just read some of your book. The guests should know why they are at your house and they would love to hear some of the book before they buy it.

THE SIGNING

People are excited when they get to meet the author of a book. When your guests are family and friends, there's an even more special bond that gets them super excited to hear about the book that you wrote. Getting a signed book from you will make them ecstatic and will make them want to talk to others about your book.

The main benefit of buying a signed book is the value that can be added to the book just by having your signature on it. Who knows...you may break out and become a best selling author and your signed books will be worth a lot more in the years to come.

When signing your book for your guests, you must consider a few things that will make your book signing very effective:

1. The Type of Pen Matters. Signing a book with a Sharpie marker may make a bold statement, but as your book ages, the felt type ink, even if it says it is permanent, will bleed and fade away. Always use a permanent ball point pen that dries immediately and will not run or bleed over time. Standard ball point pens can generally withstand getting wet and still be legible.

You want your signature to be permanent so the book will retain and gain value over time. Make sure to find pens that are "acid-free" and "archival safe". They will cost a little more money, but you won't have to worry about your signature and message fading away. And you can use them over and over again.

Always carry spare pens with you in case one runs out of ink.

2. The Pen's Color Matters. If your book is black and white all the way through, signing your book in black doesn't make it stand out. In fact, your signature can be very difficult to find. Collectors actually look for author signed books because they can get more money from them, especially after you have passed on to your next life. Use a color that stands out from your book's print so that anyone can spot it right away.

3. Pre-rehearse What You Are Going to Write. Everyone wants a little message on your book. Having book signing parties are a little more personal and will be easier to write a personalized message on a book (because you personally know them). But, if you are giving a book signing in someone else's home, you may not know all of the guests personally.

You should rehearse at least three base phrases of various lengths that you can rotate through when signing books. You will get to know them a little during the social times of your party, but you must not waste time during the signing so you can conclude the party. Try to twist some of your personal experiences with them into your signing.

4. Practice Your Signature. Your signature is a unique trait only you possess. But if you sign differently every time, then your signature is a lot more difficult to authenticate. Collectors are especially particular when it comes to an author's signature. If they have three of your books in front of them and there are slight or subtle differences between each of the signatures, that is fine. But if you have three books and you can't tell each of the signatures are yours, then you have a problem.

NEVER, EVER use your legal signature for your book signing signature. Make it different. You don't want someone using your signature and trying to steal your identity. Changing it up when you sign books will help protect your identity.

You should always practice your signature about an hour before a signing. Make sure each time you write it that you write it the same way. If you have fancy letters in your name, make sure your special motion goes into each signature so they can tell it is yours. You want to be able to sign and talk at the same time. The more you practice your signature, the better you will become at at.

5. Where You Sign Matters. The traditional area of a standard book is to sign it on the Title Page. A title page usually has a lot of white space on it and plenty of room to write a short message and sign. Don't sign a book on the cover (front or back) as these can get tattered and torn and destroy your signature. And don't hid your signature in the middle of the book somewhere. If you are signing an anthology, sign it on the first page of the story.

6. Place a Sticker. This isn't that important, but will identify your book as a signed book quickly for someone looking for it. You can purchase "Signed by Author" or "Book Signed" stickers at specialty shops that you can use or have them custom made just for you. Your sticker should be placed on the front cover of your book, preferably on the bottom right corner. Just remember not to cover your name on the book cover.

7. Always Ask the Question. You must know for certain how to spell the guest's name when signing your book. Signing a book with a message usually includes the buyer's name or a name of a family member they are buying a book for. Be sure you know how to spell their name. Don't be afraid to ask them how to spell it. There is nothing more embarrassing than signing the book for someone and the name is spelled wrong. You pretty much just trashed the book if the name is spelled wrong. There is no room for waste.

8. Date Your Signatures. Adding a date to your signature, especially within the first month after the release date will make your book even more valuable. The closer to the release date, the better. Once you start getting further from the release date, say months, then it doesn't matter as much. But I make it a habit to date all of my signatures, just so people can keep track of when they were signed.

9. Number Your Signed Books (Optional). Some authors like to limit the number of books they sign. Just remember, if you do this, your book will be more valuable because there is a limit to how many were signed, but it will also limit you on how many you can sign. If you say you are only going to sign 100 books and you number them 1/100, 2/100, 3/100, and so on, you just limited yourself on how many books you can sign during book signings. This defeats the purpose of making money during your book signings since there is no limit to how many books you can sign.

When you become more famous and your signature is worth a lot more money, then numbering your signed books may be a smart thing to do. At this point in your career, though, you don't have to worry about direct sales as much since your name is already out there and people will be looking for your books.

10. Add a Bookplate. I never knew what a bookplate was until I was writing this book, so I had to research them. Bookplates are a great personalization idea you can use to add potential value to your book. A bookplate identifies the book's owner in a fancy and traditional way. You can create these on your own printer and customize them for each guest, or you can mass order blank bookplates and add their name to them during the book signing. Bookplates can be attached with special adhesive to the inside of the front cover of the book.

11. Log All of the Books You Sign. This may seem insignificant, but knowing exactly how many books you've signed can really make a difference. Collectors love to see copy numbers attached to signatures. But if you aren't putting a copy number with your signature, you can authenticate it later with a letter stating how many signed copies were distributed. It also helps you keep track of the people that have you sign their book when you publish additional titles that may be interested in buying and have you sign as well.

The book signing is the main point of your party. Save the best for last. Once the signing is over, it is time to end the party. You can have a final word for everyone to thank them for their support. But don't drag the party on. Talk to your guests for a few minutes, but let them know you have other obligations and politely let them know they need to go.

THE MARKETING POWER OF REFERRALS
Getting Others to Hold a Book Signing Party in Their Home

As discussed earlier, it is important to think outside your home when doing book signings. Don't limit yourself just to the people you know within your network. That's what real, traditional book signings are all about. But you probably aren't ready to jump right into those just yet. In order to step further outside the box, you need to spread out from your comfort zone.

The purpose of holding a book signing in someone else's home is to get people you don't know at a book signing with the same probability of purchasing your book as your book signing at your home. You really need to tap into other people's networks to unleash the true power of the book signing, so you need to learn how to get people to host a book signing event in their home.

In network marketing companies that hold parties in people's homes, what makes them successful is the referrals from the hosts of the parties. Let's face it. You don't know everyone. You only know the people you know.

Your network may only be 250 people, but in the whole scheme of things, that isn't very many people. And only ten percent of those people may buy your book, so now you are down to 25 book sales from your immediate network. Once you exhaust all of the people you know, then what are you going to do?

Well, you could give up on the book signing parties and step way out of your box and go for a more formal, traditional book signing location where you are basically cold selling your book. Or you can tap into other people's networks – your family's networks and your friend's networks – to extend your reach.

The key to making money from book signing parties isn't in your personal network. The real money is made when you reach into other networks and expand outward.

Everyone knows 250 people in their personal network. In the book "How to Sell Anything to Anybody" by Joe Girard with Stanley H. Brown, it explains "Girard's Law of 250" in detail. Joe is known as the "world's greatest salesman" by the Guinness Book of World Records of his time. His law basically says, "Everyone knows 250 people in his or her life important enough to invite to the wedding and to the funeral – 250!"

If you really sit down and write down the names of everyone you know, as I explained in an earlier chapter, you will have a pretty good list of people. More than you thought you knew, right? Well, everyone can generate their own list of people they know, and each one of them should come up with 250 people or more, just like you did.

So, during your party, you want to ask your guests if they would like to host a book signing party in their home for their friends or family. This, of course, must be followed-up with incentives to make it more worth their while.

You will never expand outside your own home if you don't ask. If they do agree to it, you will have to meet up with them to organize and plan the party, just like you did for the one you did in your home. This is a little more difficult because it isn't in your home. Your first meeting with them will be to go over the plan and schedule, then the dreaded list.

Have them sit down and generate a list of their close friends and relatives that are local and get the invites out as soon as possible. You are in charge, but they will be hosting the party. You just need to let them know what to do and how your party will be run. You can even help with the food and beverages if they can't afford it. But you are responsible for setting it up and putting up all of the props and marketing materials.

After you get at least twenty-five people and their addresses, you will get all of the invitations ready. You will go as far as putting the invitations in envelopes, making sure they addressed correctly, and placing stamps on all of them. The person hosting the part must mail them out from their home. The point is to make the invitations look like they came from the person hosting the party. Having them do all of the writing on the invitations is a big help.

Your next meeting with them will be to make sure nothing has changed for the party and to remind them of the schedule that day. And you will be checking to see how many people RSVP'd to the invitations.

Getting people to host a party is really not as difficult as it sounds. You just have to step out of your comfort zone for a second and ask the question. Most people would love to help you out, especially if there are gifts or incentives involved.

Now let's run through an example of the power of referral marketing combined with your book signing parties.

Let's say only 5 people out of the 25 guests from the example of your network above agrees to host a book signing party for you in their home. Since each of them knows 250 people, that extends your reach out to 1,250 people. Of them, let's say ten percent agree to come to the hosted parties in other people's homes and buy books from you. That's 125 sales (of one or more books). That's five times more sales than you made from just the people you knew. Now, extending your reach even more, of those 125, say 10 want to host a book signing party for you. Now you extend your reach to 2,500 people. Of them, you make 250 sales and more referrals and book signing parties.

This can go on forever if you want. But, you must be realistic. You probably won't get that many people to agree to host a book signing event for you in their home. It would not only be difficult to do, but it just isn't going to happen like that. That was just an example. But you never know. You could have more. The point of the example is to show you the potential of referral based marketing. It compounds quickly. Don't agree to more than you can handle, but don't sell yourself short either.

I wouldn't agree to more than five parties a week once you have held at least five on your own. This will take up a lot of your time, but the rewards are well worth the effort and time involved.

Your referral marketing reach doesn't end with the parties either. Remember, you are handing out marketing materials to all of your guests. You are handing out five business cards and five post cards (at minimum) and giving everyone instructions to share these with their friends and family. Of your 25 guests that bought your book, each of them may hand out your marketing materials to 10 different people each. That's 250 potential referrals you may get just from handing out marketing materials.

I hope you see the potential here. In a more traditional book signing setting, the power of referral marketing isn't as effective because you don't know most of the people that show up and you don't have time to build a relationship enough with them in order for them to want to talk about you and your book. You will know some, but not very many. It would be very awkward to ask them to tell all of their friends and family about your book out of the blue. But when you hold a book signing party, you are more at ease and already know the people (or know the person who invited them). It's easier to ask them to help you out than a stranger.

This marketing push is optional, but highly recommended if you want to get the word out about your book and make some good money from your books.

TIPS AND SUGGESTIONS FOR
A SUCCESSFUL BOOK SIGNING PARTY

Now that you have a solid foundation for throwing a great book signing party at your home, here are some tips and other suggestions to help smooth over some of the gray areas you may encounter along the way. Every party and every situation is a little different and may call for a little extra planning.

Parties never go as planned and there are a lot of things that get thrown into the mix that you might not have anticipated in a normal mode of thinking. This chapter will give you some tips and suggestions to help alleviate some of the problems you may run into as you are setting up your parties.

Common Things to Keep in Mind Before, During and After Your Party:

1. Child Care Issues. Many people want to come to your book signing party, but many will pass on it because they have kids and can't get a sitter, or afford a sitter. If you are single, you may have a little more trouble rectifying this one, but it is still doable.

If you have a teenager, husband, or wife, offer up their services at your home to watch the guest's children while your party is taking place. Let the guests know you are going to do this so this can not be an excuse for them. Do set the rules though – no kids will be at the actually book signing party itself.

Movies are great and last just about as long as a two hour book signing party. Having lots to do for the kids in the room away from the party is a good idea too.

If you are single and have no kids, or very young kids, you may have more of a difficult time with this. You may have to hire someone to babysit for you and your guest's children, though this will take away from your profits.

If you have more than five children to watch, you should have more than one sitter. You should have one sitter for every five kids.

You can also tell your guests not to bring any children, but this will turn a few potential guest and sales away.

2. Parking. Some people don't have large areas where people can park their cars near your home, especially if you live in an apartment complex with limited parking. If you have a van, you can have your spouse pick them up at a pre-determined destination (such as a mall parking lot or nearby store parking lot). Shuttle them back and forth so the parking is not an issue. Save the spots close to your house for handicap people or people that have a more difficult time moving around.

3. Transportation. Some people will want to come to your party, but won't have a means of getting there. Offer to pick them up to bring them to your house for the party and drop them off afterwards. This is another good job for the supportive spouse or friend.

If this won't work because you are single and don't have any way of picking them up in a timely manner, offer to hold a book signing party in their home where they won't have to go anywhere.

4. Following Up With People Who Say They Can't Attend. You are going to get a lot of people who congratulate you and are excited that you wrote and published a book, but they will find every excuse under the sun to say that they can't attend your party. Some even RSVP with a yes and back out at the last minute. You must follow up with these people right away. Don't take no for an answer. They really want to come, but they may not like the social setting of the party.

Instead of pushing them to attend your book signing party, offer to go to them. Just because they may not go to your party doesn't mean you don't have to sell them a book. Be sure to bring a few books with your in case they want more than one. This just takes a little time out of your day, but you will make a sale and possibly future sales as well. Also offer to have a book signing party in their home. It doesn't hurt, but these people will probably pass on that too.

5. What Do You Do When Someone is Negative or Not Supportive? During the inviting stage, you will have people that just plain don't want to attend and don't want to buy a book. They may or may not come up with excuses, but for the most part you can tell they don't want to participate.

Negativity is something you want to stay away from when dealing with anything business, especially selling books. Negative vibes drive you down and cause you to lose your excitement and motivation. Distancing yourself from the negativity will help keep your steam going.

On the contrary, that doesn't mean they can't be your friend or family any more. Don't shove them off and forget about them. Just don't mention your book to them again. If they ask about it, they may be telling you that they are curious and had a change of heart. Then it is okay to discuss it. But other than that, they will not be contacted to attend a book signing party again.

You may also have someone turn very negative at your book signing party. Just let them be who they are. They won't be going to your table to get a book signed, so their negative influence shouldn't hurt the rest of your guests. But if they are being disruptive or verbally negative, you can ask them to leave your home. It is your home and your choice.

It's best to keep a positive attitude and handle things as professionally as possible.

6. A Guest Comes to Your Party With No Cash. There is a few ways to confront this problem. If it is a case of not having enough change on their part, you must accommodate by having enough change for everyone. Storefronts and gas station kiosks generally start their register with $150.00. Have a variety of bills to be able to accept up to $100.00 bills.

But for those people that didn't bring cash with them, you can alleviate the problem by accepting credit cards. Yes, this does cost a little money, but it doesn't have to cost money up front. And it allows more people to you're your books. Your bank or credit union may offer credit card services, but they generally charge you a monthly fee for a card reader and a service fee for each transaction.

PayPal.com, on the other hand, has a great solution for small businesses (like you). It's called PayPal Here™ and it doesn't cost you anything to get the card reader. It works with any Android Phone version 2.3.3 or later, iPhone 3GS or later, and iPad 5.0 or later. If you manually enter the credit card number, it will charge you a 3.5% fee plus $.15 per transaction, or a flat 2.7% flat rate per card swipe. The money will be deposited in your PayPal account and can easily be withdrawn to your bank account any time you like. This is the most inexpensive and simple solution for the no cash problem.

Another way, which is more hassle and paperwork for you, is to take an order on extended credit. You will need a preprinted IOU or credit receipt that you fill out with their name, address, phone, and how much they owe you. In 30 days they must pay you. The only problem with this is if they don't pay you, you have to seek out payment on your own. You will have to follow up with them, reminding them that they owe you money, and punish them for not paying you on time.

I'm more against the whole extending credit thing because it can cause tension between you and your friend/relative and this is the last thing you want in referral based marketing, or any business for that matter. If they don't pay, you can charge them a penalty fee and interest (depending on the laws within your state).

An easier way is to direct the guest to your website where they can purchase your book on the website. This can be done in your home or they can do it on their computer. Set up a special page where they buy an "author signed book". When they complete the transaction, you will get the order, sign the book for them, and send it to them or deliver it in person. If you are going to deliver it in person, you should sign it upon delivery, that way it is more personal.

7. Minimize Distractions During the Party. Distractions will disrupt your party and cause major problems if you are not careful. There's nothing worse than reading a chapter of your book and a phone rings or the doorbell rings.

Whenever the last guest arrives at your house, place a sign on the outside of your main door that says "Do Not Disturb, Book Signing in Progress". Place the sign where anyone approaching your door will see it, especially unsolicited sales people.

When your guests arrive, ask them politely to silence or shut off their mobile phones. Do the same for yours once all of your guests have arrived. Also silence or unplug the home phone line.

If you have a pet (cat or dog), lock them up in a separate room or outside. They always want to be the center of attention, especially when you have guests over, so they need to go. You can give them a treat to help out too – they won't be too mad at you. Unless of course you are promoting a book about cats or dogs and your pet was your inspiration for the story. Then they can help with the promotion.

Kids, even if they are being watched in a separate room, will want to check out what's going on. Your sitter must understand that they cannot let the children escape.

8. Dressing Appropriate for the Party. Sometimes the guests will ask what they should where to the book signing party. It's not a formal event, but don't go any less than casual. They shouldn't show up with no bra or in sweat pants. Jeans and a nice shirt, slacks, blouse, or casual dress. Clothing can be a big distraction if it is distasteful.

As far as your clothes, dress for success. You may not want to wear formal attire, but if you are a woman, wear a nice casual dress, do your hair, and put on some makeup (if you use makeup). If you are a man, wear slacks, a nice dress shirt and a tie. You don't need to wear a full suit, but men can get away with that and still look casual. You are the center of the party and you should dress like it.

9. Don't Force Marketing Materials on Your Guests. Gift bags containing marketing materials (post cards and business cards they can hand out) and other party gifts will be subtle and an easy way to help market your book without being too pushy. By handing everyone a gift bag as soon as they enter your home, you are not forcing the issue. There should be a personalized thank you note in the bag that asks them to hand out the cards to their friends and family. You can also leave a brochure in the bag to explain to them about hosting a book signing party for you in their home. This will prevent you from having to broach the issue during the party. Though in a group setting, asking everyone at the same time to help market your book or hosting a book signing party in their home is less pushy and seems more expected than a one-on-one chat with the person.

To help with your party planning, I have compiled a **Book Signing Party Planner Checklist** for you to **download**. This will help you for pre-party planning, planning just before your party, and gives you a sample schedule to help run your party from start to finish. It is in .PDF format and can be printed for your convenience.

http://www.jason-moser.com/book-signing-tools.html

CONCLUSION

A book signing party can be the most rewarding experience for an author. It not only introduces you to book marketing, it does it in a way that is not intimidating and with a lot more marketing power and reach. It also helps motivate you more because you are actually making money with your efforts. You will see that it is a fast and easy way to start making book sales and you will eventually want to expand out to a more public setting with your book signings once you get more comfortable with the who event.

Getting your name and your book's title out to as many people as possible is the name of the game in this industry, and referral based marketing is the most inexpensive and profitable way to go for authors, especially new or unknown authors.

As you hold your parties, take a lot of notes. The schedule, things you do for activities and other sales techniques may work better with your own unique twist. You will learn new things along the way.

Helping out other authors isn't a bad thing. Yes, you are in competition with them, but their product is not the same as your product. We are all in the same boat. Even if people buy a book from your competition, they will still buy a book from you just because they know the books will be totally different. There are plenty of readers to go around out there and it is not going to take away from your earnings by sharing some secrets with other writers. We are all in the same club and each of us is trying to make a living from our writing. The more sales secrets we share, the more sales we will **ALL** make.

Use Book Signing Party as your foundation for your marketing platform. Use your experience and knowledge to gain other great marketing ideas so you can make even more sales.

ABOUT THE AUTHOR

Jason Moser is a fiction and self-help author residing in Chesapeake, Virginia with his wife and two sons. He has written and self-published 2 fiction novels and several how-to and self-help book.

Jason has also written over 500 articles and content pages for his websites, some of which are no longer active.

His websites include:

www.stockmarkethacks.com
www.dinnerecipe.com
www.howtolocker.com
www.jason-moser.com

Jason's goal is to break the marketing code for self-published writers so they can reap the benefits of book sales just like the big named authors.

Book Signing Party is one huge step in that direction.

You can find all of Jason Moser's books by visiting:

www.jason-moser.com